CREATIVE COOKING COLLECTION

Party Food & Drinks

CREATIVE COOKING COLLECTION

Party Food & Drinks

Liz Downing & Pete Smith

CONTENTS

Published exclusively for Cupress (Canada) Limited
10 Falconer Drive, Unit 8, Mississauga,
Ontario L5N 1B1, Canada
by Woodhead-Faulkner Ltd

First published 1987
© Woodhead-Faulkner (Publishers) Ltd 1987
All rights reserved
ISBN 0-920691-23-4
Printed and bound in Italy by Arnoldo Mondadori Editore

INTRODUCTION

Choosing a menu for any party can be a headache. In this book we have selected ideas to cover a variety of needs—formal, informal, outdoor, large, small and simple. Select the menu best suited to the occasion, but also something that will fit in with your own time schedule; some of these menus can be prepared well in advance, while others need last-minute preparation.

Our dinner party menus serve 6–8 people. Each has a theme, with a slightly different feel and flavour. *Nouvelle cuisine* is difficult and time-consuming to present without a kitchen full of chefs, so we have created some dishes in the *nouvelle* style but with greatly simplified methods.

The main stumbling blocks to cooking for a larger function are normally deciding on how to balance a menu and the quantity of food to buy. Hot food requires more equipment, oven space and last-minute preparation so, apart from some warming snacks for 100 people, our buffet party menus are made up of a selection of cold dishes where everything can be prepared in advance.

You will, of course, be cooking in bulk, which is no more difficult than cooking for a small number but requires a little advance thought. Check that you have enough large mixing bowls to prepare the food in batches, or buy dish pans or buckets to make up the large mixtures all at once.

You may have to cook in batches, too, so make sure you have sufficient suitably sized containers and allow enough cooking time. Our times are a good guide, but if you fill the oven to capacity the dishes will take longer to cook.

We have given wine suggestions for each dinner party menu. For larger gatherings, a punch is often a good idea. Some of the punches have been designed to make the wine go further and for people who don't like drinking anything too strong, while others will help to camouflage cheaper bottles of wine. As with the wines, the punches and cocktails are provided as suggestions—any of them could be made in the desired quantity to suit your own occasion.

We have enjoyed testing these recipes on our friends and hope that this book helps you with future entertaining, making it easier and more fun.

NOTES

Ingredients are given in both metric and imperial measures. Use either set of quantities but not a mixture of both in any one recipe.

All spoon measurements are level:
1 tablespoon = one 15 ml spoon
1 teaspoon = one 5 ml spoon.

Ovens should be preheated to the temperature specified.

Freshly ground black pepper is intended where pepper is listed.

Fresh herbs are used unless otherwise stated. If unobtainable dried herbs can be substituted in cooked dishes but halve the quantities.

Eggs are large size unless otherwise stated.

DINNER PARTIES

CLASSIC DINNER PARTY

Choosing what to prepare for a dinner party can pose an awful problem. Here
we have chosen traditional dishes and added a touch of flair.

MENU FOR SIX
1st course: Cherry Soup. **Main course:** Surf and Turf, with broccoli and carrots.
Dessert: Almond Tart.

WINE SUGGESTIONS
Main course: Claret, e.g. Les Forts de Latour. **Dessert:** Sauternes, e.g. Château
Coutet.

CHERRY SOUP

398 ml (14 oz) can bing
  cherries, drained and
  pitted
600 ml (2½ cups) chicken
  stock (preferably
  homemade)
125 ml (½ cup) red wine

2 tablespoons port
1 cinnamon stick
1 thick lemon slice
TO SERVE:
125 ml (½ cup) sour
  cream

Serves 6
Preparation time:
15 minutes
Cooking time:
20 minutes
Freezing:
Recommended at
end of stage 3

1. Place the cherries, stock, wine, port, cinnamon and
lemon slice in a large saucepan. Bring to the boil and boil
rapidly for 15 minutes.
2. Discard the cinnamon and lemon slice. Allow the soup
to cool slightly.
3. Place the soup in a food processor or blender and work
until smooth.
4. Return to the saucepan and reheat. Transfer to individual soup plates and swirl a spoonful of sour cream on
each one to serve.

Illustrated top:
Surf and Turf
(page 8)

SURF AND TURF

'Surf and Turf' is a classic dish which is popular in America and Australia. Although it is rather expensive to prepare, it makes a delicious and exciting change.

*1 cooked lobster, weighing
    about 1 kg (2 lb)
300 ml (1¼ cups) white
    wine
300 ml (1¼ cups) water
50 ml (¼ cup) unsalted
    butter*

*1 tablespoon oil
6 pieces fillet steak, each
    weighing 125 g (4 oz)
2 tablespoons table cream
salt and pepper to taste
tomato roses to garnish*

Serves 6
Preparation time:
15–20 minutes
Cooking time:
About 15 minutes
Freezing:
Not recommended

Illustrated on
page 7

1. Remove all the flesh from the lobster, including the claws; these can be cracked with a hammer or ask at the fish counter for it to be done. Slice the meat from the tail and chop the remaining flesh.
2. Place the shells in a saucepan, add the wine and water and boil rapidly for about 15 minutes; strain and set aside, discarding the shells.
3. Meanwhile, melt the butter and oil in a heavy-based frying pan, add the steaks and seal quickly on both sides. Cook for 5–10 minutes, according to taste, turning once. Transfer to a warmed serving dish and keep warm.
4. Add the reserved lobster stock to the pan and boil until slightly reduced. Add the cream, lobster meat, and salt and pepper; heat through gently.
5. Place the lobster on the steaks and pour the sauce over and around them. Garnish with tomato roses and serve with broccoli and carrots.

ALMOND TART

*FOR THE PASTRY:
375 ml (1½ cups)
    all-purpose flour
125 ml (½ cup) butter
75 ml (⅓ cup) sugar
75 g (3 oz) ground
    almonds
1 egg, plus 1 yolk
2 drops almond extract
FOR THE FILLING:
50 ml (¼ cup) butter,
    softened*

*125 ml (½ cup) icing
    sugar
50 g (2 oz) ground
    almonds
2 eggs
1 tablespoon corn starch
2 teaspoons Amaretto
    liqueur or few drops
    almond extract
2 tablespoons raspberry
    jam
25 g (1 oz) sliced almonds*

1. Place all the ingredients for the pastry in a food processor and work until they just begin to hold together; if they are over-mixed at this stage the pastry will be tough.
2. Roll out the dough on a floured surface and press into a 23 cm (9 inch) fluted flan pan. Trim the edge and prick the base with a fork. Bake in a preheated oven, 200°C/400°F, for 20–25 minutes or until pale golden and firm to the touch.
3. Meanwhile, prepare the filling. Place the butter, icing sugar and ground almonds in a food processor or blender and work for about 30 seconds. Add the eggs, corn starch and Amaretto, or almond extract, and blend again until smooth.
4. Spread the base of the cooked pastry case with the jam, cover with the filling and sprinkle with the sliced almonds. Return to the oven and cook for 15 minutes or until golden brown. Serve warm or cold, with fresh raspberries and cream or yogurt if you wish.

Serves 6
Preparation time: 20 minutes
Cooking time: 35–40 minutes
Freezing: Recommended

FORMAL NOUVELLE-STYLE DINNER

This dinner party is certainly one to 'impress' but will require a certain amount of planning and some advance preparation. However, it need not be as daunting as it may at first appear.

For the best effect, each dish should be presented on fairly plain but elegant individual plates—the less intricate the decoration on the crockery the greater the impact of the food.

Try to adopt a relaxed attitude and enjoy each course to the full, savouring the individual flavours. A small pause between courses enhances the appetite.

MENU FOR SIX
1st course: Chicken Livers with Thyme. **Refresher**: Mint and Lime Granita. **Fish course**: Salmon Fillet with Fish Mousse. **Main course**: Duck Breasts with Cherry Sauce, with snow peas. **Dessert**: Ginger and Coffee Bavaroise or a selection of fresh fruit.

WINE SUGGESTIONS
1st course: white Bordeaux, e.g. Clos St Georges, Graves or Château Ferrande, or champagne. **Fish course**: white Burgundy, e.g. Chablis Premier Cru or Meursault. **Main course**: Puligny Montrachet, St Veran L. Latour or Rosemount Chardonnay. **Dessert**: Sauternes, e.g. Château Coutet or Château Rieussec.

CHICKEN LIVERS WITH THYME

75 ml (1/3 cup) butter
4 shallots, sliced thinly
2 cloves garlic, halved
1 bunch thyme
500 g (1 lb) chicken livers, halved
5 tablespoons brandy

5 tablespoons water
6 tablespoons cream
salt and pepper to taste
TO GARNISH:
cooked puff pastry shapes
thyme sprigs

Serves 6
Preparation time:
10 minutes, plus making pastry shapes
Cooking time:
12 minutes
Freezing:
Not recommended

Illustrated top right: Mint and Lime Granita (page 15)

1. Melt the butter in a large pan, add the shallots and garlic and sauté until softened, stirring with the bunch of thyme.
2. Add the chicken livers and cook for 6–7 minutes, until tender, stirring frequently. Remove the livers and keep warm.
3. Pour in the brandy and stir well, scraping up the sediment. Add the water and bring to the boil, stirring constantly with the thyme 'brush'. Boil rapidly for 2 minutes, then stir in the cream and heat through.
4. Season with salt and pepper and remove the garlic pieces and thyme brush. Pour the sauce over the livers. Garnish with puff pastry shapes and thyme to serve.

SALMON FILLET WITH FISH MOUSSE

*600 ml (2½ cups) court
    bouillon (see below)*
500 g (1 lb) halibut
150 ml (⅔ cup) white wine
*5 tablespoons whipping
    cream*
*grated peel and juice of
    1 lemon*
*150 ml (⅔ cup) egg white,
    lightly beaten*

500 g (1 lb) salmon fillet
*2 tablespoons dry
    vermouth*
*150 ml (⅔ cup) table
    cream*
2 tablespoons butter
salt and pepper to taste
TO GARNISH:
cooked asparagus spears
parsley sprigs

Serves 6
Preparation time:
30 minutes, plus
making court
bouillon
Cooking time:
15–20 minutes
Freezing:
Not recommended

1. Place the court bouillon in a pan, add the halibut and cook gently for 5–6 minutes or until the flesh has just cooked. Remove with a fish slice, reserving the court bouillon, and place in a food processor or blender. Strain the court bouillon and return to the heat. Add the white wine and simmer, uncovered, for 3–4 minutes.

2. Work the halibut until smooth. Add the whipping cream, lemon peel and juice and work until smooth. Transfer to a bowl and fold in the egg white. Add salt and pepper.

3. Cut the salmon fillet into 6 neat portions and spread the mousse over each piece. Place on a baking sheet and pour over just enough court bouillon to moisten the tin. Bake in a preheated oven, 190°C/375°F, for 15–20 minutes, until tender.

4. Meanwhile, boil the court bouillon rapidly for 10 minutes, then stir in the vermouth, table cream and butter and simmer gently for 5 minutes.

5. Remove the fish and keep warm. Stir the pan juices into the sauce. Spread the sauce over 6 plates and top each with a piece of fish. Garnish with asparagus and parsley.

To make Court Bouillon: Place 900 ml (3⅔ cups) water, 300 ml (1¼ cups) white wine, 2 tablespoons lemon juice, 1 carrot, 1 onion, a bouquet garni and 4 peppercorns in a large pan and boil for 15 minutes. Strain and use as required. This will make approximately 600 ml (2½ cups).

DUCK BREASTS WITH CHERRY SAUCE

500 g (1 lb) cherries, pitted
450 ml (1¾ cups) stock
6 duck breast fillets

5 tablespoons port
salt and pepper to taste
cherries to garnish

1. Place the cherries and stock in a pan, bring to the boil, then cover and simmer for 20 minutes or until tender. Cool slightly, then purée in a food processor or blender.
2. Place the duck breasts in a roasting pan and cook in a preheated oven, 200°C/400°F, for 35–40 minutes, until tender.
3. Reheat the cherry purée and add the port, and salt and pepper.
4. Slice each duck breast diagonally lengthways and arrange on individual serving plates. Spoon a little cherry sauce around each breast, garnish with cherries and serve immediately, with snow peas.

Serves 6
Preparation time:
45–50 minutes
Cooking time:
35–40 minutes
Freezing:
Freeze separately.
Freeze sauce at
end of stage 1

GINGER AND COFFEE BAVAROISE

4 egg yolks
75 ml (⅓ cup) sugar
175 ml (¾ cup) table
　cream
1 teaspoon vanilla extract
1 tablespoon gelatine,
　soaked in 2 tablespoons
　water
150 ml (⅔ cup) whipping
　cream, whipped
4 tablespoons strong black
　coffee
1 piece preserved ginger,
　chopped finely

4 tablespoons ginger syrup
　(from the jar of
　preserved ginger)
FOR THE COFFEE SAUCE:
300 ml (1¼ cups) strong
　black coffee
50 ml (¼ cup) sugar
1 tablespoon corn starch
4 tablespoons whipping
　cream, whipped
TO DECORATE:
2 pieces preserved ginger,
　chopped
2 tablespoons table cream

Serves 6
Preparation time:
45 minutes
Setting time:
1 hour
Freezing:
Not recommended

1. Beat the egg yolks and sugar together in a heatproof bowl until pale.
2. Heat the table cream gently to scalding point, then pour over the eggs, stirring constantly.
3. Place the bowl over a pan of simmering water and heat, stirring constantly, until the mixture thickens and coats the back of the spoon. Remove the bowl from the heat and stir in the vanilla extract.
4. Heat the gelatine gently until dissolved, then add to the custard. Carefully fold in the whipped cream, then divide the custard between 2 bowls.
5. Add the coffee to one bowl, and the ginger and syrup to the other bowl.
6. Place the bowl of coffee custard in cold water and stir until it begins to thicken but you can still pour it. Half-fill 6 small moulds with the coffee custard and chill for 30 minutes, until set.
7. Spoon the ginger custard on top and return to the refrigerator for 30 minutes, until set.
8. Meanwhile, make the coffee sauce. Place the coffee and sugar in a pan and heat gently until dissolved. Blend the corn starch with a little of the coffee, then return to the pan. Simmer, stirring, for 1–2 minutes. Leave to cool, stirring occasionally, then fold in the cream.
9. To serve, spread the coffee sauce over 6 plates. Dip the moulds, one at a time, into warm water for a few seconds, then turn out onto the sauce. Decorate with the preserved ginger and dots of cream.

MINT AND LIME GRANITA

A very pleasant way to freshen the palate between courses. It can alternatively be served as a light dessert in place of the bavaroise.

1 bottle dry white wine
2 tablespoons chopped
*   mint*
175 ml (3/4 cup) icing sugar

grated peel of 2 limes and
*   juice from 1*
mint sprigs to garnish

Serves 6
Preparation time:
10 minutes
Freezing time:
About 5 hours

1. Mix all the ingredients together and pour into a rigid freezerproof container. Cover, seal and freeze for about 5 hours.
2. To serve, scrape spoonfuls of the ice into individual glasses and garnish with mint.

Illustrated on page 11

INFORMAL NOUVELLE-STYLE DINNER

This menu, although still in the 'New Cuisine' style, is more approachable and less demanding than the previous one. Most of the food can be prepared in advance. The lightness of this meal also makes it an excellent choice for lunchtime entertaining.

MENU FOR SIX
1st course: Warm Seafood Salad. **Main course:** Sherried Noisettes with Kidneys, with zucchini and new potatoes. **Dessert:** Fruit Sorbets with Mango Coulis.

WINE SUGGESTIONS
1st course: Sauvignon Blanc or Sancerre (white). **Main course:** Claret or Burgundy, e.g. Château du Bousquet, Château Maucaillon, Château Grand Pays Ducasse or Mercurey. **Dessert:** Muscat, e.g. Beaumes de Venise, or Champagne.

WARM SEAFOOD SALAD

50 ml (¼ cup) butter
grated peel of 1 and juice
from 2 lemons
12 scallops
250 g (8 oz) scampi tails
125 ml (½ cup) white wine
2 tablespoons chopped dill
2 tablespoons whipping
cream
salt and pepper to taste

FOR THE SALAD:
heart of 1 curly endive
1 small oak leaf lettuce or
1 radicchio
125 g (4 oz) lambs' lettuce
1 small bunch chives,
chopped
TO GARNISH:
dill sprigs

Serves 6
Preparation time:
20 minutes
Freezing:
Not recommended

1. First, prepare the salad and arrange in a bowl or on 6 individual serving plates.
2. Melt the butter in a pan with a little of the lemon juice, add the scallops and scampi, and sauté until just cooked. Remove with a slotted spoon and set aside.
3. Add the remaining lemon juice, the lemon peel and wine to the pan and boil for 4–5 minutes, until reduced by half. Add the dill and cream, bring back to the boil, then turn off the heat.
4. Return the shellfish to the pan and mix well in the sauce. Check the seasoning and spoon over the salad. Garnish with dill and serve immediately.

Illustrated bottom:
Sherried Noisettes
with Kidneys
(page 18)

SHERRIED NOISETTES WITH KIDNEYS

3 lambs' kidneys, sliced
1 bunch rosemary
5 tablespoons red wine
50 ml (¹/4 cup) butter,
  clarified (see below)
6 lamb noisettes, each
  weighing 125 g
  (4 oz)

1 tablespoon redcurrant
  jelly
6 tablespoons sherry
5 tablespoons water
rosemary sprigs to garnish

Serves 6
Preparation time:
10 minutes, plus
standing time
Cooking time:
15 minutes
Freezing:
Recommended

1. Place the kidneys and rosemary in the wine and leave to stand for about 1 hour.
2. Melt the butter in a large frying pan, add the noisettes and cook for 3–4 minutes on each side, until well browned on the outside but still pink in the middle. Transfer to a warmed serving dish and keep warm.
3. Remove the kidneys from the marinade, add to the pan and fry quickly. Transfer to the serving dish.
4. Add the marinade to the pan, stirring vigorously with the bunch of rosemary to scrape up the pan juices. Add the remaining ingredients and boil rapidly for 2–3 minutes, stirring constantly with the rosemary 'brush'.
5. Spoon the sauce over the noisettes, garnish with rosemary and serve with new potatoes and zucchini.

Illustrated on
page 17

To clarify butter: Melt gently until just below simmering point and changing colour, then strain through muslin.

FRUIT SORBETS WITH MANGO COULIS

KIWI SORBET:
150 ml (²/3 cup) sugar
250 ml (1 cup) water
6 kiwi fruit, peeled
250 ml (1 cup) dry white
  wine
juice of 1 lemon
1 egg white
RASPBERRY SORBET:
150 ml (²/3 cup) sugar
250 ml (1 cup) water
500 g (1 lb) raspberries
250 ml (1 cup) dry white
  wine
1 egg white

MANGO SORBET:
4 mangoes
150 ml (²/3 cup) dry white
  wine
150 ml (²/3 cup) water
1 egg white
50 ml (¹/4 cup) sugar
MANGO COULIS:
175 ml (³/4 cup) white wine
75 ml (³/4 cup) icing sugar,
  sifted
TO SERVE:
3 tablespoons whipping
  cream
6 mint sprigs

1. For the kiwi sorbet, place the sugar and water in a small saucepan, heat gently until dissolved, then bring to the boil and boil for 1 minute. Leave to cool.

2. Purée the kiwi fruit in a food processor or blender. Strain through a fine sieve and discard the seeds.

3. Stir the wine, sugar syrup and lemon juice into the kiwi purée. Beat the egg white until stiff, then fold into the purée.

4. Turn into a rigid freezerproof container, cover and freeze for about 2 hours, until firm, stirring 3 or 4 times while freezing.

5. Make the raspberry sorbet in the same way, without lemon juice.

6. To make the mango sorbet, peel the mangoes, scrape all the flesh from the stone and purée in a food processor or blender. Measure out 300 ml (1¼ cups) of the purée; leave the rest for the mango coulis.

7. Stir the wine and water into the measured purée. Whisk the egg white until stiff, then gradually whisk in the sugar. Fold into the mango mixture. Freeze as above.

8. To make the mango coulis, add the wine and icing sugar to the reserved mango purée in the food processor or blender and work until smooth.

9. To serve, divide the coulis between 6 individual plates, spreading it out to cover the surface evenly. Arrange spoonfuls of each sorbet on the plates. Drizzle a little cream over the coulis. Decorate with the mint.

Serves 6
Preparation time:
1 hour
Freezing time:
About 2 hours

MIDWEEK DINNER PARTY

Everything in this simple menu can be prepared in advance to fit in with busy schedules—yet it is quite delicious.

MENU FOR EIGHT

1st course: Salmon and Shrimp Mousse. **Main course:** Lamb and Spinach Casserole, Potato Layer Bake. **Dessert:** Ginger and Pineapple Cake.

WINE SUGGESTIONS

1st course: Sauvignon, e.g. Pouilly Fumé. **Main course:** Châteauneuf-du-Pape.

SALMON AND SHRIMP MOUSSE

250 g (8 oz) smoked salmon pieces
500 g (1 lb) peeled shrimp
150 ml (²/₃ cup) mayonnaise (see page 48—¹/₂ quantity)
grated peel and juice of 1 lemon

3 tablespoons chopped dill
150 ml (²/₃ cup) whipping cream
2–4 drops Tabasco
50 ml (¹/₄ cup) unsalted butter, melted
TO GARNISH:
lime twists and dill sprigs

Serves 8
Preparation time: 10 minutes
Freezing: Recommended

1. Put the salmon and shrimp in a food processor and work for 30–40 seconds, until roughly chopped. Add the mayonnaise, lemon peel and juice, dill, cream and Tabasco and mix well. Stir in the cooled butter.
2. Pour into 8 ramekins and chill until required.
3. Garnish with lime and dill and serve with toast.

POTATO LAYER BAKE

1.5 kg (3 lb) potatoes, sliced thinly
350 g (12 oz) onions, sliced into rings
2 cloves garlic, crushed

2 teaspoons grated nutmeg
450 ml (1³/₄ cups) table cream
2 tablespoons butter, melted
salt and pepper to taste

Serves 8
Preparation time: 15 minutes
Cooking time: 2 hours
Freezing: Not recommended

Illustrated on page 22

1. Arrange the potato and onion in layers in a greased shallow ovenproof dish, seasoning each layer with the garlic, nutmeg, and salt and pepper; finish with potatoes.
2. Pour over the cream and cover with foil. Cook in a preheated oven, 180°C/350°F, for 1½ hours.
3. Remove the foil and brush the potatoes with the butter. Return to the oven for 30 minutes, until browned.

LAMB AND SPINACH CASSEROLE

4 tablespoons olive oil
1 large onion, chopped
1 leg of lamb, weighing
*   1.75 kg (4 lb), boned,*
*   trimmed and diced*
2 teaspoons ground
*   cinnamon*
1 teaspoon ground cumin
2 cloves garlic, crushed

50 ml (¼ cup) flour
150 ml (⅔ cup) white wine
300 ml (1¼ cups) water
2 tablespoons redcurrant
*   jelly*
250 g (8 oz) frozen
*   chopped spinach*
salt and pepper to taste

Serves 8
Preparation time:
20 minutes
Cooking time:
About 1½ hours
Freezing:
Recommended at
end of stage 3

Illustrated below
right: Potato Layer
Bake (page 20)

1. Heat the oil in a large casserole, add the onion and
sauté until softened.
2. Add the lamb, spices and 1 clove garlic and fry, stirring
frequently, until the meat is browned all over.
3. Stir in the flour, then gradually add the wine and water.
Bring to the boil, cover and cook in a preheated oven,
180°C/350°F, for about 1½ hours, until tender.
4. Return the casserole to the top of the stove and add the
remaining garlic, the redcurrant jelly and spinach. Bring
back to the boil and season with salt and pepper. Simmer
gently for 5 minutes. Serve immediately.

GINGER AND PINEAPPLE CAKE

*300 ml (1 1/4 cups)
  all-purpose flour*
1/2 teaspoon baking soda
1/2 teaspoon salt
*2 teaspoons ground
  cinnamon*
2 teaspoons ground ginger
1 teaspoon grated nutmeg
1 egg, beaten
3 tablespoons molasses

*150 ml (2/3 cup) sour
  cream*
*50 ml (1/4 cup) butter,
  melted*
FOR THE TOPPING:
50 ml (1/4 cup) butter
*150 ml (2/3 cup) dark
  brown soft sugar*
*398 ml (14 oz) can
  pineapple slices, drained*
*25 g (1 oz) preserved
  ginger, shredded*

1. First, make the topping. Melt the butter in a small pan, add the sugar and stir over a gentle heat for 1–2 minutes, until dissolved. Pour into a 23 cm (9 inch) round cake pan. Arrange the pineapple and ginger in it.
2. Sift the dry ingredients into a bowl. Mix the remaining ingredients together, stir into the dry ingredients and beat well to make a smooth batter.
3. Pour over the fruit and bake in a preheated oven, 180°C/350°F, for 45 minutes.
4. Turn onto a warmed dish. Serve with whipped cream.

Serves 8
Preparation time:
15 minutes
Cooking time:
45 minutes
Freezing:
Not recommended

ITALIAN DINNER PARTY

A meal in true Italian style—this is not one for dieters. Save up your calories to indulge in this menu!

MENU FOR EIGHT
1st course: Pasta with Mushroom Sauce. **Main course**: Stuffed Veal Rolls, Radicchio and Fennel Salad, Potato and Zucchini Fritto. **Dessert**: Cassata Bombe.

WINE SUGGESTIONS
1st course: Frascati Amabile. **Main course**: Barolo Riserva Speciale.

PASTA WITH MUSHROOM SAUCE

50 ml (¼ cup) butter
1 large onion, sliced thinly
2 large cloves garlic, crushed
350 g (12 oz) mushrooms, sliced
2 large red peppers, cored, seeded and sliced

300 ml (1¼ cups) table cream
2 × 250 g (8 oz) packets fresh green and white pasta shells
salt and pepper to taste
basil leaves to garnish

Serves 8
Preparation time:
10 minutes
Cooking time:
8 minutes
Freezing:
Recommended for sauce only

1. Melt the butter in a pan, add the onion and garlic and sauté gently until softened. Add the mushrooms and peppers, stir well and cook for 5 minutes.
2. Add the cream, plenty of pepper and some salt and heat through gently.
3. Meanwhile, cook the pasta according to packet directions. Drain and arrange on a warmed serving dish. Pour over the sauce and serve immediately, garnished with basil.

RADICCHIO AND FENNEL SALAD

2 small radicchio, broken into small pieces
1 bulb fennel, sliced thinly

1 tablespoon olive oil
2 tablespoons lemon juice
salt and pepper to taste

Serves 8
Preparation time:
10 minutes
Freezing:
Not recommended

1. Arrange the radicchio and fennel in a serving bowl.
2. Mix the oil and lemon juice together, season with salt and pepper, and pour over the salad just before serving.

POTATO AND ZUCCHINI FRITTO

750 g (1½ lb) potatoes	1 teaspoon salt
750 g (1½ lb) zucchini	1 teaspoon pepper
300 ml (1¼ cups) flour	1 teaspoon mustard
3 tablespoons finely	powder
chopped parsley	2 egg whites, whisked
1 tablespoon finely	lightly
chopped rosemary	oil for shallow-frying

Serves 8
Preparation time:
15 minutes, plus
standing time
Cooking time:
About 20 minutes
Freezing:
Not recommended

1. Cut the potatoes and zucchini into large chips. Boil the potatoes in boiling salted water for 5–7 minutes until almost cooked, then drain and refresh under cold water.
2. Mix together the flour, herbs and seasonings.
3. Dip the vegetable chips into the egg white, then coat with the seasoned flour. Leave to stand for 15 minutes.
4. Shallow-fry in batches in hot oil for 4–6 minutes, until golden and crispy. Serve immediately.

STUFFED VEAL ROLLS

8 veal escalopes, beaten	125 ml (½ cup) fresh
2 tablespoons butter	breadcrumbs
2 tablespoons oil	1 large clove garlic
300 ml (1¼ cups) dry	50 g (2 oz) Parmesan
white wine	cheese, in pieces
juice of ½ lemon	large bunch basil leaves
150 ml (⅔ cup) table	3 tablespoons olive oil
cream	TO GARNISH:
salt and pepper to taste	basil leaves
FOR THE STUFFING:	shredded lemon peel
50 g (2 oz) pine nuts	

Serves 8
Preparation time:
25 minutes
Cooking time:
About 40 minutes
Freezing:
Recommended at
end of stage 1

1. First make the stuffing. Place all the ingredients in a blender or food processor and work until smooth. Spread over the veal, roll up and secure with string.
2. Heat the butter and oil in a large pan, add the veal rolls and fry gently until browned all over, turning constantly. Transfer to a shallow ovenproof dish.
3. Add the wine to the pan, stirring well to scrape up the sediment. Boil rapidly until reduced by half, then add the lemon juice, cream, and salt and pepper.
4. Pour over the veal, cover and cook in a preheated oven, 180°C/350°F, for 40 minutes, or until tender.
5. Arrange the veal rolls on a warmed serving dish, pour over the sauce and garnish with basil and lemon peel.

CASSATA BOMBE

Although this seems a long and complicated recipe, it can be prepared well in advance and the end result is quite stunning. To serve, turn out onto a serving plate and cut into slices with a hot knife.

FOR THE BASIC CUSTARD
   ICE CREAM:
550 ml (2¼ cups) table
   cream
4 egg yolks
125 ml (½ cup) sugar
FOR THE CHERRY ICE
   CREAM:
398 ml (14 oz) can bing
   cherries, drained and
   pitted
125 ml (½ cup) icing
   sugar
1 tablespoon lemon juice
300 ml (1¼ cups)
   whipping cream,
   whipped

FOR THE CASSATA ICE
   CREAM:
125 g (4 oz) crystallized
   fruits, chopped
2 tablespoons brandy
125 ml (½ cup) whipping
   cream, whipped
1 drop almond extract
FOR THE PISTACHIO ICE
   CREAM:
125 g (4 oz) pistachio nuts
1 tablespoon Amaretto
   liqueur or 2 drops
   vanilla extract
125 ml (½ cup) whipping
   cream, whipped
few drops green food
   colouring

Serves 8–10
Preparation time:
2½–3 hours
Freezing time:
About 4 hours
Freezing:
Recommended for
2–3 months

1. To make the basic custard ice cream, heat the cream gently to simmering point. Beat the egg yolks and sugar together until thick and pale in colour. Gradually pour on the hot cream, stirring constantly.
2. Strain into a heavy-based or double boiler and cook gently, stirring constantly, until the custard coats the back of the spoon; do not allow to boil.
3. Pour into a large bowl and cool. Transfer to a rigid freezerproof container, cover and freeze for about 1½ hours, until half frozen. Beat 3 or 4 times during freezing.
4. To make the cherry ice cream, purée the cherries in a food processor or blender. Add the icing sugar and lemon juice, then fold in the cream. Transfer to a rigid freezerproof container, cover and freeze for 2 hours, beating after 1 hour.
5. Soak the crystallized fruit in the brandy for 1 hour.
6. Chop 50 g (2 oz) of the pistachios roughly and grind the other 50 g (2 oz) in a blender or food processor.
7. Whisk the half-frozen custard ice cream with a fork and divide in half. Fold the fruit and brandy, cream and almond extract into one half for the cassata ice cream. Fold the

pistachios, liqueur or extract, cream and food colouring into the other half for the pistachio ice cream.

8. Return both ice creams to the freezer for about 1½ hours, beating at least once after about 1 hour.

9. Chill a 1.75 litre (7 cup) bombe mould or pudding bowl for about 1 hour in the freezer.

10. Remove the cherry ice cream from the freezer and leave to soften slightly. Use to cover the inside surface of the bombe mould or bowl in an even layer, pressing it well against the side. Return to the freezer for about 30 minutes, until set.

11. Remove the pistachio ice cream from the freezer and leave to soften slightly. Use to line the mould, covering the cherry ice cream to an even depth all over. Return to the freezer for about 30 minutes, until set.

12. Finally, fill the centre of the mould with the cassata ice cream; this will be slightly softer in texture than the others. Press well into the mould. Cover, seal and freeze for about 1 hour.

13. Transfer to the refrigerator 30 minutes before serving to soften.

INDIAN DINNER PARTY

Meat is not a major ingredient in Indian cooking. Using vegetables and pulses you can create an exciting and perfectly balanced feast, as shown here. Serve the meal with lager or chilled white wine, or even water or tea.

MENU FOR EIGHT
Poppadoms, Vegetable Kofta Curry, Dhal and Spinach Bhaji, plus accompaniments.

VEGETABLE KOFTA CURRY

250 g (8 oz) parsnips, chopped roughly
250 g (8 oz) carrots, chopped roughly
350 g (12 oz) potatoes, diced
2 large cloves garlic
large piece fresh ginger root
1 egg, beaten
6–8 tablespoons all-purpose flour
1 tablespoon cumin seeds
oil for shallow frying
FOR THE CURRY SAUCE:
2 tablespoons oil
2 tablespoons butter

2 onions, sliced
3 cloves garlic, sliced thinly
3.5 cm (1½ inch) piece fresh ginger root, chopped finely
1 green chilli, chopped finely
2 tablespoons garam masala
3 tablespoons tomato paste
600 ml (2½ cups) water
175 ml (¾ cup) thick yogurt
salt to taste
TO GARNISH:
lime twists

Serves 8
Preparation time:
35–45 minutes
Cooking time:
20 minutes
Freezing:
Not recommended

1. Cook the vegetables with the garlic, ginger and salt in boiling water until tender. Drain and remove the ginger.
2. Purée the vegetables in a food processor or blender. Add the egg and enough flour to make a smooth dropping consistency.
3. Fry the cumin seeds in a minimum of oil until they begin to split. Add to the vegetable purée.
4. Heat some oil in a frying pan and drop in spoonfuls of the purée. Fry on both sides until golden, drain on paper towels, place on a warmed serving dish and keep warm.
5. To make the sauce, heat the oil and butter in a pan, add the onion and sauté until softened. Add the garlic, ginger and chilli and fry for 2 minutes. Stir in the garam masala, then add the tomato paste and blend in the water. Season with salt, bring to the boil, then simmer for 15 minutes.
6. Add the yogurt and bring back to the boil. Pour over the koftas and garnish with lime to serve.

SPINACH BHAJI

2 tablespoons butter	1 kg (2 lb) frozen leaf
3 tablespoons oil	spinach, thawed, or
2 large onions, sliced	1.75 kg (4 lb) fresh
1 large green chilli,	spinach, blanched
chopped finely	4 cloves garlic, crushed
2 teaspoons ground	
coriander	

Serves 8
Preparation time:
10 minutes
Cooking time:
About 10 minutes
Freezing:
Not recommended

1. Heat the butter and the oil in a large pan. Add the onion and fry until softened. Add the chilli and coriander and cook for 2–3 minutes.
2. Add the spinach and garlic and cook for 4–5 minutes, until heated through. Transfer to a warmed serving dish and serve immediately.

DHAL

2 tablespoons oil	5 cardamom pods
1 onion, chopped	5 cloves
2 cloves garlic, sliced thinly	1 cinnamon stick
2 tablespoons ground	500 g (1 lb) masoor dhal
cumin	(red lentils)
1 tablespoon turmeric	1.2 litres (5 cups) water
1 tablespoon ground	75 g (3 oz) creamed
coriander	coconut
1 teaspoon hot chilli	salt to taste
powder	cinnamon stick to garnish

Serves 8–10
Preparation time:
10 minutes
Cooking time:
About 1 hour
Freezing:
Not recommended

1. Heat the oil in a pan, add the onion and garlic and fry until softened. Add the spices and cook for 2–3 minutes, stirring constantly.
2. Add the dhal and water, cover and simmer for about 50 minutes, until tender.
3. Add salt and more liquid if required, then stir in the creamed coconut in pieces. Bring back to the boil to heat through, then transfer to a warmed serving dish. Garnish with a cinnamon stick and serve immediately.

CHINESE DINNER PARTY

This quick-to-prepare Chinese-style meal is perfect for spontaneous entertaining. If your budget won't run to Sake, serve good China tea.

MENU
1st course: Cream of Corn Soup. **Main course:** Chow Mein, Egg Fu Yung.

CREAM OF CORN SOUP

Serves 8
Preparation time:
5 minutes
Cooking time:
10 minutes
Freezing:
Recommended

2 × 284 ml (10 oz) cans
creamed corn
341 ml (12 oz) can kernel
corn

400 ml (1²⁄₃ cups) water
4 tablespoons dry sherry
4 green onions, shredded
salt and pepper to taste

Put all the ingredients in a pan, bring slowly to the boil, then simmer gently for about 10 minutes. Serve hot.

CHOW MEIN

500 g (1 lb) egg noodles
4 tablespoons oil
2.5 cm (1 inch) piece fresh
ginger root, chopped
finely
3 cloves garlic, sliced
1 green chilli, chopped
finely
250 g (8 oz) each leeks,
carrots and zucchini,
sliced into matchsticks

1 red pepper, cored, seeded
and sliced
6 celery sticks, sliced
1 head Chinese cabbage,
chopped
398 ml (14 oz) can baby
corn cobs, drained
900 ml (3²⁄₃ cups) water
150 ml (²⁄₃ cup) dry sherry
4 tablespoons soy sauce
2 tablespoons corn starch

Serves 8
Preparation time:
30 minutes
Cooking time:
12–15 minutes
Freezing:
Not recommended

1. Cook the noodles according to packet directions.
2. Heat the oil in a wok or deep frying pan, add the ginger, garlic and chilli; fry for 30 seconds. Add the leeks, carrots, zucchini, red pepper and celery; stir-fry for 4 minutes.
3. Remove half of the vegetables with a slotted spoon. Add the drained noodles to the pan and stir-fry for 3 minutes. Transfer to a large warmed serving dish and keep warm.
4. Return the remaining stir-fried vegetables to the pan with the Chinese cabbage and baby corn and stir-fry for 3 minutes. Transfer to the serving dish.
5. Mix together the remaining ingredients and pour into the pan. Cook, stirring, until thick and glossy. Pour over the vegetables, toss well and serve immediately.

EGG FU YUNG

3 tablespoons sesame oil
4 green onions, chopped finely
250 g (8 oz) button mushrooms, sliced

6 eggs, beaten
2 tablespoons chopped coriander leaves
salt and pepper to taste

1. Heat 1 tablespoon of the oil in a large heavy-based frying pan, add the green onions and cook for 1 minute. Add the mushrooms and cook for 1–2 minutes. Transfer to a bowl and leave to cool slightly.

2. Add the eggs, coriander, and salt and pepper; mix well.

3. Heat the remaining oil in the pan, pour in the egg mixture and cook gently for 6–8 minutes, until firm, moving the uncooked egg about in the pan with a spatula to cook through. If the top is slightly soft, place under a preheated broiler until firm. Serve immediately.

Serves 8
Preparation time: 15 minutes
Cooking time: 8–11 minutes
Freezing: Not recommended

BARBECUE PARTY

Barbecues can be simple and traditional—sausages, burgers, chops and salads—or as exciting as any gourmet feast. Include sausages and burgers with this menu if you wish—especially if children are present—and add baked potatoes and roasted corn on the cob as well as, or instead of, the salads. The Citrus Sour Cream Mayonnaise is perfect with baked potatoes, while the relish and chutney are ideal with sausages, burgers, chops and steaks. The Apricot Lamb Chops and Swordfish Kebabs can be cooked under a traditional broiler if the weather is bad. The cooking times given are an approximate guide only—it will depend on the heat of your barbecue. To drink, the Citrus Wine Cup is not too intoxicating and could be drunk all day. The Sangria has a little more punch!

MENU FOR TWENTY
Swordfish Kebabs, with Citrus Sour Cream Mayonnaise, Apricot-Glazed Lamb Chops, sausages and/or burgers or steaks with Tomato and Raisin Chutney and Cucumber Relish, Beet Salad, Bean and Zucchini Salad.
Dessert: Baked Bananas with Chocolate, and a selection of fresh fruit.

Drink Suggestions: Sangria, Citrus Wine Cup.

SWORDFISH KEBABS

These are ideal for a barbecue. Any firm-textured fish can be used, e.g. shark, tuna or monk fish.

50 g (2 oz) fresh ginger root, grated
juice of 2 limes
175 ml (¾ cup) sunflower oil
2 large cloves garlic, crushed

1.75 kg (4 lb) swordfish, skinned, boned and cut into 2.5 cm (1 inch) cubes
4 limes, sliced
salt and pepper to taste
coriander leaves to garnish

Makes 20
Preparation time: 10 minutes, plus marinating
Cooking time: about 10 minutes
Freezing: Not recommended

Illustrated top right: Citrus Wine Cup (page 42)

1. Mix together the ginger, lime juice, oil, garlic, and salt and pepper and pour over the fish. Leave in the refrigerator for at least 8 hours, or overnight.
2. Thread 20 skewers alternately with fish and lime.
3. Place on the barbecue grid and cook for about 10 minutes, turning frequently and basting with the marinade, until tender.
4. Transfer to a serving platter and garnish with coriander. Serve with Citrus Sour Cream Mayonnaise (page 40).

TOMATO AND RAISIN CHUTNEY

This chutney can be made in advance and kept in the refrigerator for at least a week before using. Cover tightly with plastic wrap, or place in a screw-top jar. It is a good accompaniment for sausages and any plain meat.

4 tablespoons red wine
4 tablespoons wine vinegar
4 tablespoons water
125 g (4 oz) raisins

2 teaspoons mild chilli powder
750 g (1½ lb) tomatoes, skinned and chopped
1 bunch green onions, chopped

Serves 20
Preparation time:
20 minutes
Cooking time:
10–15 minutes
Freezing:
Not recommended

1. Place the wine, vinegar, water and raisins in a pan and simmer gently for 10–15 minutes or until the liquid is almost absorbed. Stir in the chilli powder.
2. Mix the tomatoes and green onions together, then stir in the raisin mixture. Leave to cool before serving.

APRICOT-GLAZED LAMB CHOPS

175 g (6 oz) dried apricots
2 teaspoons coriander seeds, crushed
3 large cloves garlic, crushed
2 tablespoons chopped coriander leaves

300 ml (1¼ cups) olive or vegetable oil
5 tablespoons lemon juice
20 lamb chops
salt and pepper to taste
coriander leaves to garnish

Serves 20
Preparation time:
40 minutes, plus marinating
Cooking time:
10–15 minutes
Freezing:
Recommended at end of stage 3

1. Place the apricots, coriander seeds and 2 tablespoons water in a pan, bring slowly to the boil, then cover and simmer for 15–20 minutes, until the apricots are tender. Leave to cool slightly, then purée in a blender or food processor.
2. Add the garlic, chopped coriander, oil and lemon juice and season well with salt and pepper.
3. Pour the apricot marinade over the chops, turning to coat well. Cover and chill for at least 8 hours or overnight.
4. Lift the chops from the marinade with a slotted spoon and place on the barbecue grid. Cook for 10–15 minutes, turning and basting once with the marinade, until tender.
5. Garnish the chops with coriander. Serve the remaining marinade separately, warm or cold, if you wish.

CUCUMBER RELISH

*½ cucumber, chopped
    roughly*
1 teaspoon salt

*250 g (8 oz) dill pickles,
    chopped roughly*
2 teaspoons chopped mint

1. Sprinkle the cucumber with the salt and leave to stand in a sieve for 30 minutes, to drain away excess moisture.
2. Place the cucumber, dill pickles and mint in a food processor or blender and work for 20–30 seconds to produce a rough purée.
3. Turn into a small bowl and chill until required. Serve with sausages and any plain meat.

Serves 20
Preparation time:
10 minutes, plus standing time
Freezing:
Not recommended

BEET SALAD

1.5 kg (3 lb) raw beet,
    peeled and grated
    coarsely
250 g (8 oz) celery, sliced
250 g (8 oz) apples, cored
    and sliced

300 ml (1¼ cups) mayon-
    naise (see page 48)
150 ml (⅔ cup) sour
    cream
4 tablespoons creamed
    horseradish
salt and pepper to taste

Serves 20
Preparation time:
20 minutes
Freezing:
Not recommended

1. Mix together the beet, celery and apple.
2. Blend the mayonnaise with the sour cream and horser-adish. Season with salt and pepper and stir into the beet mixture. Mix well before serving.

BEAN AND ZUCCHINI SALAD

4 tablespoons olive oil
1 kg (2 lb) zucchini, sliced
2 large cloves garlic,
    crushed
500 g (1 lb) green beans,
    halved

2 × 398 ml (14 oz) cans
    red kidney beans,
    drained and rinsed
salt and pepper to taste

Serves 20
Preparation time:
20 minutes
Freezing:
Not recommended

1. Heat the oil in a large pan, add the zucchini and garlic and cook, stirring occasionally, until just tender. Transfer to a salad bowl.
2. Blanch the green beans in boiling salted water for 3–4 minutes, drain and refresh under cold water. Toss into the zucchini with the kidney beans, and salt and pepper.

CITRUS SOUR CREAM MAYONNAISE

This can be served with the Swordfish Kebabs (page 36), baked potatoes, cold meats, fish or salads.

**Makes about 1
litre (4 cups)**
Preparation time:
15 minutes
Freezing:
Not recommended

Illustrated on
page 37

600 ml (2½ cups)
    mayonnaise (see below)
250 ml (1 cup) sour cream

grated peel and juice of
    1 lemon, 1 lime and
    1 orange
salt and pepper to taste

1. Make the mayonnaise as directed on page 48, using 1 egg plus 1 yolk, and doubling the remaining ingredients.
2. Stir in the sour cream, fruit peels and juice, and season with salt and pepper.

CITRUS WINE CUP

1.5 litres (6 cups) white wine
600 ml (2½ cups) lemonade

600 ml (2½ cups) soda water
5 lemons, sliced thinly

Makes 16 glasses
Preparation time:
5 minutes

Mix all the ingredients together in a large punch bowl and chill well before serving. Serve with extra ice.

SANGRIA

Any seasonal fruits, or fruits of your choice, can be used.

1.5 litres (6 cups) red wine
5 tablespoons Cointreau
    or Grand Marnier
600 ml (2½ cups)
    lemonade

600 ml (2½ cups) soda
    water
2 oranges
2 apples
¼ cucumber
few mint sprigs

Makes 16 glasses
Preparation time:
5 minutes

Place all the ingredients in a large punch bowl, floating the mint on top. Chill well before serving.

BAKED BANANAS WITH CHOCOLATE

These are absolutely delicious! Although this may seem a fairly small quantity of sauce, it is very rich and only a little is needed with each banana. It could also be served with various ice creams and sundaes.

175 ml (¾ cup) butter
175 ml (¾ cup) cocoa
    powder
125 ml (½ cup) golden
    syrup

250 ml (1 cup) table cream
few drops vanilla extract
20 bananas

Serves 20
Preparation time:
5 minutes
Cooking time:
About 10 minutes
Freezing:
Not recommended

1. Melt the butter in a pan, then stir in the cocoa powder. Add the syrup and cream and bring to the boil, then cook gently for about 5 minutes. Stir in the vanilla extract.
2. Meanwhile, place the unpeeled bananas on the barbecue grid for about 10 minutes, until the skins are black.
3. To serve, make a slit along the length of the bananas with a knife, insert about 2 teaspoons chocolate sauce and eat with spoons out of the skin.

PICNIC PARTY

You've always wanted to do the summer season in style—now you can! Pack your hamper with these ideas and you'll be the envy of the day. The combination of champagne and peach juice—a 'Bellini'—is the ultimate accompaniment to this summer fare.

MENU FOR TEN
Coulibiac, Chicken Surprise, Vegetables à la Grecque and Bacon, Chive and Potato Salad. **Dessert:** Cheese and Fruit Flan.

COULIBIAC

600 ml (2½ cups) milk
500 g (1 lb) smoked haddock
75 ml (⅓ cup) butter
125 ml (½ cup) flour
500 g (1 lb) leeks, sliced thinly

4 hard-boiled eggs, chopped coarsely
500 g (1 lb) packet puff pastry
salt and pepper to taste
beaten egg to glaze

Serves 10
Preparation time:
40 minutes
Cooking time:
40 minutes

1. Place the milk in a pan, add the fish and cook gently for 10–15 minutes, until tender. Remove the fish, reserving the liquor. Remove the skin and bones and flake the fish.
2. Melt 50 ml (¼ cup) of the butter in a pan and stir in the flour. Remove from the heat and gradually add the fish liquor. Return to the heat and bring to the boil, stirring constantly, until thickened. Set aside.
3. Melt the remaining butter in another pan, add the leeks and 1 tablespoon water, cover and cook for 5 minutes or until softened.
4. Stir the fish, leeks and eggs into the white sauce, season with salt and pepper and leave to cool.
5. Roll out the pastry to a rectangle 30 × 38 cm (12 × 15 inches). Spread the fish mixture over one half of the rectangle, leaving a 2.5 cm (1 inch) border round the edges of the pastry. Brush all the pastry edges with beaten egg and fold over the uncovered half to enclose the filling. Seal the edges well.
6. Make a lattice pattern on top of the pastry, using a sharp knife, and brush with beaten egg. Place on a baking sheet and bake in a preheated oven, 200°C/400°F, for 20 minutes. Lower the heat to 170°C/325°F, and bake for a further 20 minutes.
7. Leave until cold. Wrap in foil to take to the picnic. Cut into slices to serve.

Illustrated top:
Bellini, 2 parts
champagne to
1 part peach juice
Illustrated bottom
left: Bacon, Chive
and Potato Salad
(page 48)

VEGETABLES À LA GRECQUE

3 tablespoons olive oil
1 onion, chopped
1 teaspoon chopped
oregano
1 teaspoon chopped basil
2 cloves garlic, crushed
350 g (12 oz) button
mushrooms
350 g (12 oz) zucchini,
sliced

2 tablespoons tomato paste
398 ml (14 oz) can
chopped tomatoes
4 tablespoons red wine
300 g (10 oz) fresh or
frozen broad beans
salt and pepper to taste

Serves 10
Preparation time:
10 minutes
Cooking time:
10–15 minutes
Freezing:
Recommended

1. Heat the oil in a pan, add the onion and cook until softened. Add the herbs, garlic, mushrooms and zucchini and fry for 3–4 minutes, stirring frequently.
2. Add the tomato paste, tomatoes, wine and broad beans. Simmer for 8 minutes, or until the vegetables are tender. Add salt and pepper and leave to cool.
3. Transfer to a rigid container to take to the picnic.

CHICKEN SURPRISE

Boning out a bird for stuffing is a fairly complicated process and takes time but it is well worth it.

1.75 kg (4 lb) chicken,
boned (see note)
1 kg (2 lb) guinea fowl,
boned (see note)
FOR THE STUFFING:
50 ml (¼ cup) butter
1 onion, chopped
finely

grated peel and juice of
1 lemon
2 tablespoons chopped
thyme
250 ml (1 cup) fresh
breadcrumbs
salt and pepper to taste

1. First, prepare the stuffing. Melt the butter in a pan, add the onion and sauté until softened. Stir in the remaining ingredients, then set aside to cool.
2. Lay the chicken out skin side down so that it is completely flat. Lay the guinea fowl on top, skin side down. Spread the stuffing over the meat and season with a little extra salt and pepper.
3. Roll into a neat sausage shape so that the line of the original breast bone runs down the length on top of the roll. Tuck in the ends and sew up with fine string and a trussing needle. Brush lightly with oil.

4. Place in a baking dish and cook in a preheated oven, 190°C/375°F, for about 1½ hours, until tender.

5. Place on a board and leave to cool, then chill well in the refrigerator. Pack in a rigid container to take to the picnic. Cut into slices to serve.

Note: The best way to learn how to bone out a bird is to get someone else to show you how to do it or follow a good step-by-step guide.

Begin by cutting the bird along the centre of the back, open out flat and scrape the flesh from the back bone, using a very sharp knife. Snip the sinews at the wing joints and free the bone, scraping the flesh from the bone and turning the wings inside out as you do. Repeat with the legs. Finally remove the carcass.

Serves 10
Preparation time: 30 minutes
Cooking time: About 1½ hours
Freezing: Recommended

BACON, CHIVE AND POTATO SALAD

12 bacon slices
1 teaspoon Dijon mustard
1 tablespoon vinegar
2 tablespoons oil
1.5 kg (3 lb) unpeeled new
    potatoes, boiled, halved
    if large
large bunch chives,
    chopped

FOR THE MAYONNAISE:
1 egg
1 teaspoon Dijon mustard
1/2 teaspoon salt
1 tablespoon lemon juice
300 ml (1 1/4 cups)
    sunflower oil

Serves 10
Preparation time:
20–25 minutes,
plus cooking
potatoes
Freezing:
Not recommended

Illustrated on
page 45

1. Cook the bacon under a preheated broiler until browned and crisp. Drain on paper towels, then crumble into small pieces.
2. Mix the mustard with the vinegar and oil, add the potatoes and toss well. Leave to cool.
3. To make the mayonnaise, place the egg, mustard, salt and lemon juice in a food processor or blender and work for 45 seconds.
4. With the machine running, gradually add the oil in a steady stream, until the mayonnaise is thick and creamy.
5. Mix the mayonnaise into the potatoes, then sprinkle with the crumbled bacon and chives.
6. Transfer to a rigid container to take to the picnic.

CHEESE AND FRUIT FLAN

The pastry can be prepared and cooked in advance, but for best results the case should not be filled and topped until the day it is required. The pastry can also be prepared and frozen uncooked.

FOR THE PASTRY:
500 ml (2 cups)
    all-purpose flour
125 ml (1/2 cup) butter
125 ml (1/2 cup) sugar
4 egg yolks
grated peel of 2 lemons
FOR THE FILLING:
350 g (12 oz) light cream
    cheese
50 ml (1/4 cup) sugar
6 tablespoons thick yogurt

1 tablespoon lemon juice
150 ml (2/3 cup) whipping
    cream, whipped
FOR THE TOPPING:
2–3 nectarines, sliced
    thinly
250 g (8 oz) strawberries,
    halved
8 tablespoons apricot jam,
    sieved
2 tablespoons lemon juice

1. Place the pastry ingredients in a food processor and blend until just combining. Remove and knead lightly to make a firm dough. Chill for at least 30 minutes.

2. Roll out the pastry and use to line a 30 cm (12 inch) loose-bottomed flan ring. Line with foil and half-fill with dried beans. Bake 'blind' in a preheated oven, 190°C/375°F, for 30–40 minutes. Remove the foil and beans and leave to cool.

3. Meanwhile, prepare the filling. Cream together the soft cheese and sugar in a bowl. Stir in the yogurt and lemon juice, then fold in the cream.

4. Fill the pastry case with the cream cheese filling and arrange the fruit on top.

5. Heat the jam and lemon juice gently until thick and syrupy. Brush over the fruit, coating well.

6. Take to the picnic in a rigid container, or place on a board, cover with foil or plastic wrap and pack carefully.

Serves 10–12
Preparation time: 45 minutes, plus chilling
Cooking time: 30–40 minutes
Freezing: Not recommended

BUFFET PARTIES

FINGER FOOD PARTY

This is a very versatile menu. You may decide to choose a few ideas for a small drinks party, or serve them all for a slightly more formal cocktail party. The complete menu would serve 20–25 people. All the food can be prepared well in advance so there's no excuse for hiding in the kitchen!

MENU

Fried Nuts, Marinated Olives, Seafood Balls and Fried Shrimp with Smoked Oyster Dip, Chicken Filo Parcels, Fried Cheese Canapés, Spiced Raw Beef Balls with Chilli Dip, Lamb Meat Balls with Garlic Dip, Cheese and Herb Straws.

Drink Suggestions: Kir Punch, Strawberry Shrub.

FRIED NUTS

*2 tablespoons unsalted
    butter*
2 tablespoons vegetable oil
*500 g (1 lb) mixed
    unsalted nuts, e.g.*

*brazils, cashews,
    peanuts, almonds,
    hazelnuts*
1/2 teaspoon salt

Serves 12–15
Cooking time:
5–7 minutes
Freezing:
Not recommended

1. Melt the butter and oil in a large frying pan, add the nuts and fry for 5–7 minutes, stirring, until golden.
2. Remove from the pan and drain on paper towels. Sprinkle with salt and serve warm or cold.

MARINATED OLIVES

These will keep for up to 3 weeks in a cool dark cupboard.

GREEN OLIVES:
500 g (1 lb) green olives
*2 tablespoons chopped
    coriander leaves*
*1 tablespoon crushed
    coriander seeds*
3 cloves garlic, crushed
*grated peel and juice of
    1 lemon*

olive oil to cover
BLACK OLIVES:
500 g (1 lb) black olives
1 large onion, sliced thinly
*1/2 each red and green
    chilli, chopped finely*
*2 teaspoons Italian dried
    herbs*
olive oil to cover

Serves 25
Preparation time:
15 minutes
Freezing:
Not recommended

Illustrated top: Kir
Punch (page 58)

Place the olives and their seasonings in separate screw-top jars and cover with olive oil. Leave in a cool place for at least 24 hours before serving.

SMOKED OYSTER DIP

2 × 105 g (3½ oz) cans
    smoked oysters, drained
125 g (4 oz) carton cream
    cheese

150 ml (⅔ cup) table
    cream
3 tablespoons mayonnaise
pepper to taste

Serves 25
Preparation time:
5 minutes
Freezing:
Not recommended

1. Place the oysters in a food processor or blender. Add the remaining ingredients and work until smooth.
2. Serve with either of the recipes below or crudités.

FRIED SHRIMP

20 raw large shrimp
3 tablespoons dry sherry
2 tablespoons soy sauce
4 tablespoons water

grated peel and juice of
    1 lemon
2 cloves garlic, crushed
1 teaspoon sugar

Serves 20
Preparation time:
15 minutes, plus
marinating
Cooking time:
3–5 minutes
Freezing:
Not recommended

1. Remove the shells from the shrimp, leaving on the tail shells. Remove the dark vein running along the back of the shrimp. Rinse and drain on paper towels.
2. Mix the remaining ingredients in a large bowl, add the shrimp and leave to marinate for at least 1 hour.
3. Remove from the marinade and stir-fry in a lightly oiled non-stick pan over a high heat for 3–5 minutes, to cook. Serve hot or cold with Smoked Oyster Dip (above).

SEAFOOD BALLS

500 g (1 lb) haddock,
    skinned
500 g (1 lb) peeled shrimp
1 teaspoon anchovy paste
pinch of grated nutmeg

150 ml (⅔ cup) whipping
    cream
4 egg whites
1.2 litres (5 cups) hot fish
    stock
salt and pepper to taste

Serves 20–25
Preparation time:
10 minutes
Cooking time:
20 minutes
Freezing:
Not recommended

1. Place the haddock, shrimp, anchovy paste, nutmeg, and salt and pepper in a blender or food processor and work until smooth. Slowly add the cream and egg whites and blend until smooth.
2. Using a large fluted nozzle, pipe 2.5 cm (1 inch) lengths into the fish stock. Simmer gently for 3–4 minutes.
3. Remove with a slotted spoon; drain on paper towels.
4. Serve warm or cold with Smoked Oyster Dip (above).

CHICKEN FILO PARCELS

5 tablespoons olive oil	*2 tablespoons chopped*
500 g (1 lb) boneless	*parsley*
chicken, chopped finely	*3 tablespoons thick yogurt*
1 large onion, chopped	*75 ml (⅓ cup) butter*
finely	*400 g (14 oz) packet filo*
grated peel of 1 lemon	*pastry*
250 g (8 oz) Feta cheese,	*salt and pepper to taste*
crumbled	

Makes 36
Preparation time:
50 minutes
Cooking time:
35 minutes
Freezing:
Recommended

1. Heat 2 tablespoons of the oil in a pan, add the chicken and onion and fry gently for 15 minutes. Transfer to a bowl and leave to cool slightly.
2. Add the lemon peel, cheese, parsley and yogurt and stir well.
3. Melt the butter with the remaining oil.
4. Lay out 3 sheets of filo pastry, brush generously with the melted butter and oil, then place them on top of each other. Cut each into 9 oblongs by making 3 cuts along the length and 3 along the width of the pastry. Lay them out on the work surface.
5. Place a teaspoon of filling in the centre of each, then fold up like a parcel. Place on a baking sheet with the joins tucked underneath. Repeat with the remaining pastry and chicken mixture.
6. Brush the parcels with any remaining melted butter and oil and bake in a preheated oven, 190°C/375°F, for 35 minutes or until golden.
7. Serve warm or cold.

FRIED CHEESE CANAPÉS

1 large loaf thick-sliced	*250 g (8 oz) ripe blue brie*
white bread, crusts	*cheese*
removed	*oil for shallow-frying*

Makes 60
Preparation time:
25 minutes
Cooking time:
5 minutes
Freezing:
Not recommended

1. Roll out the bread with a rolling pin to flatten.
2. Spread a thin layer of blue brie onto each slice, then roll up tightly like a jelly roll.
3. Cut each roll into 3 pieces and shallow-fry in batches over a high heat for 1 minute. Remove with a slotted spoon and drain on paper towels.
4. Serve warm or cold.

SPICED RAW BEEF BALLS

The raw steak must be absolutely fresh and these meat balls should be eaten on the day they are made.

1 small onion	*few drops Tabasco*
2 tablespoons capers	*500 g (1 lb) fillet or rump*
25 g (1 oz) dill pickle	*steak, cubed*
50 g (1¾ oz) can anchovy	*1 egg yolk*
fillets, drained	*salt and pepper to taste*

Makes 20
Preparation time:
15 minutes, plus
chilling
Freezing:
Not recommended

1. Place the onion, capers, dill pickle, anchovies and Tabasco in a food processor or blender and chop roughly. Add the beef and work for a few seconds, until roughly chopped.
2. Stir in the egg yolk, and salt and pepper. Roll into small balls and place on a serving plate. Cover with plastic wrap and chill well. Serve with Chilli Dip (below).

CHILLI DIP

1 each red and green	*500 g (1 lb) tomatoes,*
pepper, halved and	*skinned and seeded*
seeded	*1 clove garlic*
1 red chilli, seeded	*1 teaspoon wine vinegar*
½ small onion	*salt and pepper to taste*

Serves 25
Preparation time:
30 minutes
Freezing:
Not recommended

1. Place the peppers, skin side up, under a preheated broiler for about 20 minutes, turning occasionally, until the skins are blackened. Peel under running cold water.
2. Place the peppers, chilli, onion, tomatoes and garlic in a food processor or blender and work until smooth.
3. Stir in the vinegar, and salt and pepper.
4. Serve with prepared raw vegetables, or meat balls.

CHEESE AND HERB STRAWS

These will keep for about a week in an airtight container.

750 ml (3 cups)	*pinch of salt*
all-purpose flour	*175 ml (¾ cup) butter*
1 teaspoon cayenne pepper	*500 ml (2 cups) grated*
1 teaspoon dry mustard	*old Cheddar cheese*
1 tablespoon mixed dried	*1 egg, beaten*
herbs	

1. Sift the flour into a bowl, add the cayenne, mustard, herbs and salt and mix well.
2. Rub in the butter until the mixture resembles fine breadcrumbs, then stir in the cheese. Bind the mixture together with the egg.
3. Roll out the dough on a floured surface and cut into 7.5 × 1 cm (3 × ½ inch) strips. Twist and place on baking sheets. Bake in a preheated oven, 220°C/425°F, for 10–15 minutes, until golden. Serve warm or cold.

Makes 70–80
Preparation time:
20 minutes
Cooking time:
10–15 minutes
Freezing:
Not recommended

STRAWBERRY SHRUB

'Shrubs' make a delicious change to orange juice when mixed with champagne or sparkling wine. Ideal for children, too—simply mix with lemonade or soda water instead. They will keep for about a week in the refrigerator.

1.5 kg (3½ lb) strawberries
sugar (see below)
citric acid

TO SERVE:
1.5 litres (6 cups)
    champagne or sparkling
    white wine

Makes about 20 glasses
Preparation time:
1 hour
Cooking time:
15 minutes

1. Place the strawberries in a pan and bring slowly to the boil, stirring constantly to crush the fruit. Simmer for 5–10 minutes, until pulpy.
2. Strain through a fine piece of muslin or a jelly bag.
3. Measure the strained juice into a clean pan and add 300 ml (1¼ cups) water, 375 ml (1½ cups) sugar and 1 teaspoon citric acid to each 600 ml (2½ cups) fruit juice. Heat gently until the sugar has dissolved.
4. Pour into bottles, cover and chill.
5. To serve, mix the strawberry shrub with the champagne or sparkling wine.

VARIATION
Apricot and Almond Shrub: Replace the strawberries with apricots. Add ½ teaspoon almond extract at stage 3.

KIR PUNCH

Makes 20 glasses
Preparation time:
5 minutes

1.5 litres (6 cups) white
    wine
175 ml (¾ cup) Cassis

5 tablespoons brandy
1.2 litres (5 cups) soda
    water

Illustrated on
page 51

Mix all the ingredients together in a large punch bowl. Serve well chilled.

GARLIC DIP

Serves 25
Preparation time:
5 minutes
Freezing:
Not recommended

480 g (1 lb 1 oz) thick
    yogurt
grated peel and juice of
    ½ lemon

2 cloves garlic, crushed
    with a little salt
salt and pepper to taste

Combine all the ingredients and stir until smooth.

LAMB MEAT BALLS

1 kg (2 lb) ground lamb
1 large onion, chopped
  finely
4 cloves garlic, crushed
50 g (2 oz) coriander
  leaves, chopped
  finely

2 teaspoons ground cumin
250 g (8 oz) black olives,
  pitted and chopped
1 egg yolk
1½ teaspoons salt
1 teaspoon pepper
oil for deep-frying

Makes about 50
Preparation time:
20 minutes
Cooking time:
About 15 minutes
Freezing:
Recommended

1. Combine all the ingredients and roll into small balls.
2. Deep-fry in hot oil, in batches, for 5–6 minutes, until golden. Remove with a slotted spoon and drain on paper towels. Serve hot or cold, with Garlic Dip (opposite).

BUFFET PARTY FOR 30

This menu could also be served as a formal sit-down supper party.
The Grapeshot is perfect as an aperitif and to drink throughout the meal.

MENU

1st course: Salmon and Avocado Mousse. **Main course:** Beef Niçoise with Mixed
Leaf Salad and Potatoes Salsa Verde. **Desserts:** Lime and Passion Soufflé,
Hazelnut Mocha Gâteau or a selection of fresh fruit.

Drink Suggestion: Grapeshot.

SALMON AND AVOCADO MOUSSE

SALMON MOUSSE:
4 × 220 g (7³/4 oz) cans
   red salmon
milk (see below)
50 ml (¹/4 cup) butter
125 ml (¹/2 cup) flour
2 teaspoons anchovy paste
1 tablespoon tomato paste
450 ml (1³/4 cups) mayon-
   naise (see page 48)
3 envelopes gelatine
   soaked in 1 tablespoon
   lemon juice and
   8 tablespoons water

AVOCADO MOUSSE:
6 ripe avocados
3 tablespoons lemon juice
300 ml (1¹/4 cups)
   mayonnaise (see page
   48)
125 ml (¹/2 cup) whipping
   cream
2 envelopes gelatine
   soaked in 6 tablespoons
   water
salt and pepper to taste
TO GARNISH:
watercress sprigs
cooked shrimp in shell

Serves 30
Preparation time:
40 minutes
Setting time:
About 2 hours
Freezing:
Not recommended

Illustrated top left:
Grapeshot
(page 64)

1. Drain the liquid from the salmon and make up to
600 ml (2½ cups) with milk.
2. Melt the butter in a pan, stir in the flour, then blend in
the milk mixture. Bring to the boil, stirring, then cool.
3. Purée the salmon in a food processor or blender. Add
the anchovy paste, tomato paste, cooled white sauce and
mayonnaise, and work until evenly mixed.
4. Heat the gelatine gently until dissolved. Stir into the
salmon mixture. Season with salt and pepper.
5. Divide the mixture between two 1.75 litre (7 cup) ring
moulds. Chill for about 1 hour, until set.
6. Purée the avocados in a food processor or blender; add
the lemon juice, mayonnaise and cream. Heat the gelatine
gently until dissolved, then mix into the avocado mixture,
with salt and pepper. Pour onto the salmon; chill until set.
7. To serve, dip the moulds briefly into hot water and turn
out the mousses. Garnish with watercress and shrimp.

MIXED LEAF SALAD

1 curly endive
2 radicchio
350 g (12 oz) lambs' lettuce
2 oakleaf lettuce
2 romaine lettuce

2 bunches watercress
2 boxes nasturtium flowers
* (optional)*
juice of 2 lemons

Serves 30
Preparation time:
10 minutes
Freezing:
Not recommended

1. Place the salad leaves and nasturtiums, if using, in a large bowl and toss well to mix.
2. Pour over the lemon juice just before serving.

BEEF NIÇOISE

To save time, the beef can be cooked a day in advance. It is best cooked rare as this adds to the flavour of the dish.

1.75 kg (4 lb) beef
* tenderloin*
4 egg plants
3 each red and green
* peppers, cored, seeded*
* and skinned (see*
* page 56)*
2 tablespoons oil
2 cloves garlic, crushed
1 kg (2 lb) zucchini, sliced

12 tomatoes, skinned and
* quartered*
500 g (1 lb) black olives
FOR THE DRESSING:
350 ml (1½ cups) olive oil
4 cloves garlic, crushed
juice of 3 lemons
salt and pepper to taste

Serves 30
Preparation time:
45 minutes, plus
standing time
Cooking time:
1¼ hours
Freezing:
Not recommended

1. Roast the beef in a preheated oven, 190°C/375°F, for 1¼ hours. Leave until cool.
2. Meanwhile, prepare the remaining ingredients. Slice the egg plants, sprinkle with salt and place in a colander. Weight down lightly and leave for about 1 hour to drain.
3. Slice the skinned peppers into strips and place in a large bowl. Heat the oil and garlic in a frying pan, add the zucchini and fry for 3–4 minutes, until just softened. Remove with a slotted spoon and add to the peppers. Add the tomatoes and mix well.
4. Wash the egg plants under running cold water, then drain well. Reheat the frying pan, add the sliced egg plants a few at a time and cook for 4–5 minutes, until beginning to brown. Add to the bowl and mix well.
5. Mix the dressing ingredients together, then pour over the vegetables.
6. Cut the meat into fine strips, add to the vegetables with the olives and mix well.

POTATOES SALSA VERDE

4 hard-boiled eggs
150 g (5 oz) parsley
2 × 50 g (1¾ oz) cans
    anchovy fillets, drained
6 large cloves garlic
600 ml (2½ cups) olive oil

.300 ml (1¼ cups)
    vegetable oil
4.5 kg (10 lb) unpeeled
    new potatoes, boiled
salt and pepper to taste
parsley sprigs to garnish

Serves 30
Preparation time:
15 minutes, plus
cooking potatoes
Freezing:
Not recommended

1. Place the eggs, parsley, anchovies and garlic in a food processor or blender and work until smooth. Gradually add the oils and blend until thick. Add salt and pepper.
2. Pour over the hot potatoes. Serve hot or cold, garnished with parsley.

GRAPESHOT

2 litres (8 cups) rosé wine
600 ml (2½ cups) red
    grape juice

125 ml (½ cup) brandy
125 g (4 oz) black grapes
2 bottles dry sparkling
    white wine

Makes 30 glasses
Preparation time:
5 minutes

Illustrated on
page 61

1. Place the rosé wine, grape juice, brandy and grapes in a large bowl and chill well.
2. Just before serving, pour in the sparkling wine.

LIME AND PASSION SOUFFLÉ

12 eggs, separated
375 ml (1½ cups) sugar
10 limes
175 ml (¾ cup) water

4 envelopes gelatine
10 passion fruit, halved
1.2 litres (5 cups) whipping
cream, whipped

1. Whisk the egg yolks and sugar together with an electric beater until thick and creamy.
2. Grate the peel from 8 limes; set aside one quarter for decoration. Squeeze the juice from all 10 limes.
3. Pour 5 tablespoons of the lime juice and the water into a small pan. Sprinkle on the gelatine and leave for about 5 minutes, until spongy.
4. Remove the flesh and seeds from the passion fruit and add to the egg mixture with the grated lime peel and remaining juice. Fold in three quarters of the cream.
5. Heat the gelatine gently until dissolved, then add to the mousse mixture, stirring thoroughly.
6. Whisk the egg whites until stiff, then gently fold into the mousse mixture, using 2 bowls if necessary.
7. Pour the mixture into two 1.75 litre (7 cup) soufflé dishes and chill for about 2 hours, until set.
8. Pipe the reserved cream around the edges of the soufflés and sprinkle over the reserved lime peel.

Serves 30
Preparation time:
30 minutes
Setting time:
About 2 hours
Freezing:
Not recommended

HAZELNUT MOCHA GÂTEAU

FOR THE CAKE:
500 ml (2 cups) butter
500 ml (2 cups) sugar
8 eggs
1 litre (4 cups) self-
raising flour, sifted
175 g (6 oz) hazelnuts,
toasted and ground
1 tablespoon instant coffee
granules
6 tablespoons warm milk
FOR THE SHORTBREAD:
250 ml (1 cup) butter
125 ml (½ cup) sugar
250 g (8 oz) hazelnuts,
toasted and ground
600 ml (2½ cups)
all-purpose flour

FOR THE FILLING:
150 ml (⅔ cup) water
150 ml (⅔ cup) very
strong black coffee
200 g (7 oz) plain
chocolate, broken into
pieces
1.2 litres (5 cups) whipping
cream, whipped
8 tablespoons black cherry
jam
TO DECORATE:
50 g (2 oz) hazelnuts,
toasted
50 g (2 oz) chocolate
caraque (see opposite)

Makes two 25 cm (10 inch) gâteaux
Preparation time: 1 hour 20 minutes
Cooking time: 55–65 minutes
Freezing: Recommended

1. Grease and line two 25 cm (10 inch) round cake pans.
2. Beat the butter with the sugar until light and fluffy. Add the eggs one at a time, adding about a tablespoon of flour with each egg and beating well between each addition.
3. Combine the ground hazelnuts with the remaining flour and add half to the creamed mixture.
4. Dissolve the coffee in the milk, then fold into the mixture. Add the remaining flour mixture and stir well.
5. Turn the mixture into the prepared pans and bake in a preheated oven, 180°C/350°F, for 45–50 minutes, until firm to the touch and shrunk slightly away from the side of the pans. Turn onto wire racks to cool.
6. Place all the shortbread ingredients in a food processor and work to form a smooth dough. Wrap in plastic wrap and chill for at least 30 minutes.
7. Divide the dough in half and press each piece evenly over the base of a 25 cm (10 inch) spring form cake pan.
8. Bake in a preheated oven, 190°C/375°F, for 10–15 minutes. Leave to cool in the pans.
9. To make the filling, place the water and coffee in a pan, add the chocolate and heat gently until melted. Leave to cool slightly, then fold into the cream.
10. Place each piece of shortbread on a serving plate and cover with jam.
11. Cut each cake in half horizontally and place one round on each piece of shortbread.

12. Cover with cream and top with the remaining cake.
13. Spread the remaining cream over the top and side of each cake. Decorate with the hazelnuts and chocolate caraque.

To make chocolate caraque: Melt the chocolate and pour onto a cold surface. Leave until set but not hard. Using a sharp thin-bladed knife at a slight angle, scrape the chocolate off with a slight sawing movement to form long thin scrolls.

BUFFET PARTY FOR 50

It may seem a daunting task setting about cooking for large numbers but it needn't be. Organization is the key word to success. Yes, the dishes do need to be larger—there's nothing wrong with mixing in clean dish pans!

MENU

Pork and Pistachio Terrine, Seafood Salad, Chicken in Green Sauce, Tomato and Onion Salad, Mustard Seed Potatoes, Cauliflower and Snow pea Salad, Mixed Bean and Pepper Salad. **Desserts:** Frozen Chocolate Pudding, Fruit Salad.

WINE SUGGESTIONS

Champagne or Saumur and Château la Borie or red and white Bergerac.

PORK AND PISTACHIO TERRINE

1.5 kg (3 lb) ground pork
1 kg (2 lb) belly pork,
  skinned and ground
350 g (12 oz) pork liver,
  ground
2 Spanish onions, chopped
  finely
2 cloves garlic, crushed

1½ teaspoons ground
  mace
3½ teaspoons salt
1½ tablespoons coarse
  grain mustard
75 ml (⅓ cup) sherry
175 g (6 oz) shelled
  pistachio nuts
salt and pepper to taste

Serves about 30
Preparation time:
15 minutes, plus
standing time
Cooking time:
1½ hours
Freezing:
Recommended

1. Mix all the ingredients together and place in two 2 L (9 × 5 inch) loaf pans. Cover with a double piece of foil and place in a roasting pan half-filled with hot water.
2. Cook in a preheated oven, 180°C/350°F, for 1½ hours. Leave to cool in the pan for an hour, then stack one on top of the other, place a heavy weight on top and leave in a cool place for 8 hours. Turn out and slice thinly.

TOMATO AND ONION SALAD

2.25 kg (5 lb) tomatoes
350 g (12 oz) small onions

5 oranges
salt and pepper to taste

Serves 50
Preparation time:
15 minutes, plus
standing time
Freezing: ·
Not recommended

1. Slice the tomatoes and onions thinly into rings.
2. Grate the peel from 3 of the oranges and squeeze the juice from all 5 oranges.
3. Layer the tomatoes, onions and orange peel in two large serving dishes, seasoning each layer with salt and pepper.
4. Pour over the orange juice, cover and leave in a cool place for 2 hours before serving.

SEAFOOD SALAD

1 kg (2 lb) swordfish steaks	*500 g (1 lb) peeled shrimp*
1 tablespoon oil	*2 red peppers, cored,*
50 g (2 oz) shallots, sliced	*seeded and sliced*
thinly	*salt and pepper to taste*
1 clove garlic, crushed	*FOR THE MARINADE:*
1 kg (2 lb) monkfish, cut	*juice of 2 lemons*
into bite-size pieces	*4 tablespoons oil*
1 kg (2 lb) squid, sliced	*1 clove garlic, crushed*
into rings	*3–4 parsley stalks*
500 g (1 lb) scallops, sliced	*TO GARNISH:*
500 g (1 lb) large shrimp	*dill sprigs*

Serves 25–30
Preparation time:
45–50 minutes,
plus marinating
Cooking time:
20–25 minutes
Freezing:
Not recommended

1. Mix the marinade ingredients together, add the swordfish and leave for 1 hour, turning occasionally.
2. Heat the oil in a large heavy-based frying pan, add the shallots and garlic and fry for 1–2 minutes, until soft but not brown. Increase the heat, add the monkfish and cook over high heat for 4–5 minutes, stirring constantly. Remove the monkfish with a slotted spoon and place in a large bowl.
3. Add the squid to the pan and cook for 1–2 minutes. Remove with a slotted spoon and add to the monkfish.
4. Add the scallops to the pan and cook for 2–3 minutes. Remove with a slotted spoon and add to the bowl. Take the pan off the heat.
5. Remove the shells and heads from the large shrimp, reserving the shells. Slice the flesh and add to the other fish with the peeled shrimp.
6. Blanch the peppers in boiling salted water for 2 minutes. Strain and add to the fish.
7. Remove the swordfish from the marinade and cook under a preheated broiler for 7–10 minutes, until tender. Flake the fish and add to the bowl.
8. Pour the marinade into a pan and add the reserved shrimp shells. Boil rapidly for 2–3 minutes, then strain. Add to the fish, mix well and season with salt and pepper. Cool before serving.
9. Garnish with dill to serve.

MUSTARD SEED POTATOES

*170 g (6 oz) jar English
  vineyard seed mustard
4 large cloves garlic,
  crushed
6 tablespoons lemon juice
6 tablespoons white wine
  vinegar
300 ml (1 1/4 cups) olive oil*

*150 ml (2/3 cup) vegetable
  oil
5.5 kg (12 lb) new
  potatoes, boiled
3 bunches green onions,
  chopped
salt and pepper to taste*

1. Mix the mustard and garlic together, stir in the lemon juice and vinegar, then gradually blend in the oils. Season with salt and pepper.
2. Toss the potatoes in the dressing while they are still hot, using two bowls if necessary. Leave to cool.
3. Transfer to 2 large serving bowls, sprinkle with the green onions and mix well.

Serves 50
Preparation time:
10 minutes, plus cooking potatoes
Freezing:
Not recommended

CAULIFLOWER AND SNOW PEA SALAD

6 cauliflowers broken into florets	*350 ml (1½ cups) vegetable oil*
1 kg (2 lb) snow peas	*1 clove garlic, crushed*
FOR THE DRESSING:	*½ teaspoon salt*
175 ml (¾ cup) white wine vinegar	*½ teaspoon sugar*
	pepper to taste

Serves 50
Preparation time:
20 minutes
Freezing:
Not recommended

1. Cook the cauliflower and snow peas separately in boiling salted water for about 5 minutes, so that they are still crunchy. Drain and refresh in cold water.
2. Mix the dressing ingredients together, pour over the vegetables and mix well. Transfer to 2 large serving bowls.

CHICKEN IN GREEN SAUCE

Poaching the chickens in a court bouillon (see page 12) will keep the meat moist. However, if this seems too time-consuming they can be roasted in the normal way.

2 tablespoons oil	*300 ml (1¼ cups) water or*
250 g (8 oz) frozen spinach, thawed	*chicken stock (approximately)*
2 cloves garlic, crushed	*4 chickens, each weighing*
1 teaspoon grated nutmeg	*2.25 kg (5 lb), cooked*
3 bunches watercress	*salt and pepper to taste*
25 g (1 oz) parsley	*watercress to garnish*
1.2 litres (5 cups) mayonnaise (see page 48)	

Serves 30–35
Preparation time:
1 hour, plus
cooking chickens
Freezing:
Not recommended,
though the
chickens can be
cooked and frozen
in advance

Illustrated top:
Mixed Bean and
Pepper Salad
(page 74)

1. Heat the oil in a pan, add the spinach and garlic and sauté for about 5 minutes, until the spinach is heated through. Season with the nutmeg and leave to cool.
2. Discard most of the stalks from the watercress, place in a food processor or blender with the parsley and work until well chopped. Add the spinach and continue blending, adding a little of the mayonnaise, to make a thick, smooth purée.
3. Add the remaining mayonnaise and blend well. Thin with water or chicken stock to the desired consistency. Season well with salt and pepper.
4. Remove the chicken meat and cut into pieces. Place in a large bowl, pour over the sauce and mix well. Transfer to serving dishes and garnish with watercress.

MIXED BEAN AND PEPPER SALAD

*3 × 398 ml (14 oz) cans
red kidney beans
3 × 398 ml (14 oz) cans
white kidney beans
2 yellow and 1 green
pepper, cored, seeded
and diced*

*FOR THE DRESSING:
2 cloves garlic, crushed
1 tablespoon each tomato
ketchup and Dijon
mustard
2 tablespoons creamed
horseradish
6 tablespoons wine vinegar
225 ml (7/8 cup) oil
50 g (2 oz) parsley, chopped
salt and pepper to taste*

Serves 50
Preparation time:
15 minutes
Freezing:
Not recommended

Illustrated on
page 73

1. First prepare the dressing. Mix the garlic, ketchup, mustard and horseradish together in a bowl, add the vinegar, then gradually blend in the oil. Season with salt and pepper, then add the parsley.
2. Drain and rinse all the beans, mix with the diced peppers, then toss well in the dressing.
3. Transfer to 2 large serving bowls.

FROZEN CHOCOLATE PUDDING

*12 egg whites
750 ml (3 cups) fine sugar
1 kg (2 lb) plain cooking
chocolate, broken into
pieces
150 ml (2/3 cup) brandy*

*150 ml (2/3 cup) water
1.5 litres (6 cups) whipping
cream, whipped lightly
250 g (8 oz) walnuts,
chopped roughly*

Serves 50
Preparation time:
35 minutes
Cooking time:
2½–3 hours
Freezing time:
3–4 hours

1. Line 1 or 2 baking sheets with non-stick parchment.
2. Whisk the egg whites until stiff. Gradually whisk in half of the sugar, then fold in the rest. Spread onto the baking sheet(s) and bake in a preheated oven, 120°C/250°F, for 2½–3 hours. Crush roughly.
3. Place the chocolate, brandy and water in a pan and heat gently until melted. Leave to cool slightly.
4. Fold three quarters of the chocolate into the cream. Mix well, then fold in the meringue and walnuts.
5. Pour in the remaining chocolate and mix lightly to create a marbled effect. Pour into a foil-lined 5.5 litre (22 cup) capacity roasting pan, cover, seal and freeze for 3–4 hours, until firm.
6. Transfer to the refrigerator 15 minutes before serving to soften slightly. Cut into slices to serve.

FRUIT SALAD

1.75 g (4 lb) strawberries, halved	*8 peaches or nectarines, sliced thinly*
1.5 kg (3 lb) raspberries	*150 ml (²/₃ cup) kirsch*
1 kg (2 lb) blackberries	*sugar to taste*

Place all the fruit in a large bowl, sprinkle with the kirsch and sugar, cover and leave in a cool place for at least 30 minutes.

Note: If you cannot obtain fresh raspberries or blackberries, use frozen ones.

Serves 50
Preparation time:
30 minutes, plus
standing time
Freezing:
Not recommended

BOTTLE PARTY FOR 100

Here are a few ideas for all those wild parties where the drink is more important than the food! Punches help to make the drink go further, and are a good way to use up the cheap 'plonk' that's usually brought to a bottle party. Any of the punches given in this book can be served. They all take only a few minutes to prepare and can be easily made while the party's in full swing. Just make sure you've got a few other ingredients to add to the wine!

FRENCH BREAD PIZZA

175 ml (³⁄₄ cup) olive oil
3 large Spanish onions,
chopped roughly
1 tablespoon Italian dried
herbs
4 large cloves garlic,
crushed
156 ml (5¹⁄₂ oz) can
tomato paste

5 × 540 ml (19 oz) cans
peeled tomatoes
5 French sticks, halved
lengthways
2 kg (4¹⁄₂ lb) Mozzarella
cheese, sliced thinly
75 g (3 oz) Parmesan
cheese, grated
pepper to taste

Serves 100
Preparation time:
30 minutes
Cooking time:
20 minutes
Freezing:
Recommended for
the sauce only

1. Heat the oil in 1 or 2 large pans, add the onions and sauté until softened. Add the herbs and garlic and cook for 2–3 minutes.
2. Stir in the tomato paste and the tomatoes with their juice, bring to the boil, then simmer for 7–10 minutes or until the sauce is fairly thick. Leave to cool.
3. Spread the sauce generously over the halved French sticks, then cover with the Mozzarella cheese. Season with a little pepper and sprinkle with Parmesan cheese.
4. Place on baking sheets and bake in a preheated oven, 200°C/400°F, for about 20 minutes, until the cheese is golden and bubbling.
5. Cut each half stick into 10 pieces and serve at once.

TROPICAL WINE PUNCH

3 litres (12 cups) white
wine
400 ml (1²⁄₃ cups) dark
rum
4 litres (16 cups) tropical
fruit juice

2 × 398 ml (14 oz) cans
pineapple chunks in
natural juice
1 × 250 ml (8 oz) jar
maraschino cherries

Makes 50 glasses
Preparation time:
5 minutes

Combine all the ingredients in a large bowl and chill well.

SAUSAGE MEAT PLAIT

175 g (6 oz) sage and onion stuffing mix	*2.75 kg (6 lb) sausage meat*
450 ml (1¾ cups) boiling water	*4 × 500 g (1 lb) packets puff pastry*
1.25 kg (2½ lb) cooking apples, peeled, cored and grated	*2 eggs, beaten, to glaze salt and pepper to taste*

Makes about 70 small slices
Preparation time:
30 minutes
Cooking time:
45 minutes
Freezing:
Recommended

1. Mix the stuffing with the boiling water, add the grated apple and leave to cool.
2. Mix in the sausage meat and season well with salt and pepper.
3. Roll out the pastry on a floured surface into 4 rectangles, 50 × 25 cm (20 × 10 inches). Place a quarter of the stuffing down the centre of each rectangle. Using a sharp knife, make 1 cm (½ inch) slashes down each long side of the pastry. Brush with beaten egg, tuck the two ends in and fold alternate strips from each side over the filling to form a long plait.
4. Brush well with beaten egg and bake in a preheated oven, 200°C/400°F, for 45 minutes. Serve hot or cold.

DEVILLED CHICKEN DRUMSTICKS

2 tablespoons mustard powder	*1 tablespoon pepper*
2 tablespoons ground cumin	*2 tablespoons ground ginger*
2 tablespoons chilli powder	*1 tablespoon ground cinnamon*
2 tablespoons turmeric	*3 tablespoons paprika*
3 tablespoons ground coriander	*250 ml (1 cup) flour*
3 tablespoons salt	*50 ml (¼ cup) sugar*
	100 chicken drumsticks

Makes 100
Preparation time:
10 minutes, plus standing time
Cooking time:
About 1 hour
Freezing:
Recommended

1. Mix all the dry ingredients together in a large bowl and use to coat the chicken pieces; if you do not have anything large enough to mix them in, use a clean plastic bin liner. Leave to stand for at least 1 hour.
2. Arrange the chicken pieces on oiled baking sheets and cook in a preheated oven, 200°C/400°F, for about 1 hour, until tender.
3. Serve hot or cold.

MULLED WINE

6 litres (25 cups) red wine
1 litre (4 cups) water
9 oranges, cut into small
    pieces

4 cinnamon sticks
500 g (1 lb) sugar
    (approximately)
175 ml (¾ cup) Grand
    Marnier or Cointreau

1. Place the wine, water, oranges, cinnamon sticks and half of the sugar in a large pan and heat gently until the sugar has dissolved.
2. Add the liqueur, taste and add more sugar if required: this will vary according to the wine you have used as a base and your own taste.
3. Pour into a punch bowl and serve hot.

Makes 50 glasses
Preparation time:
20 minutes

INDEX

Photography by: Paul Williams
Designed by: Sue Storey
Home economists: Liz & Pete
Stylist: Penny Markham
Illustrated by: Linda Smith
Typeset by Rowland Phototypesetting Ltd